The Lord Is My Shepherd!

from
PSALM 23

by Joel Anderson

illustrated by Kristi Carter & Joel Anderson

 A Golden Book • New York

Golden Books Publishing Company, Inc.
New York, New York 10106

Dedicated to Hannah Faith Baggett, age 6,
and her family, Doyle, Daniela, & Sarah Grace Baggett

Even though I walk through the valley of the shadow of death,
I will fear no evil, for you are with me… Psalm 23:4

"As Hannah's family, we have walked with her through this
valley of sickness, acute lymphocytic leukemia, without
regard of what the outcome may be. Through hope and faith,
we have found green pastures and still waters for the journey."

Scripture for dedication taken from the HOLY BIBLE, NEW INTERNATIONAL VERSION.
Copyright © 1973, 1978, 1984 by International Bible Society. Used by permission of Zondervan
Publishing House.

The Lord is my shepherd.
I have everything I need.

He lets me rest in the cool grass.

He leads me by the quiet stream.

He gives me strength and He guides me to the right path.

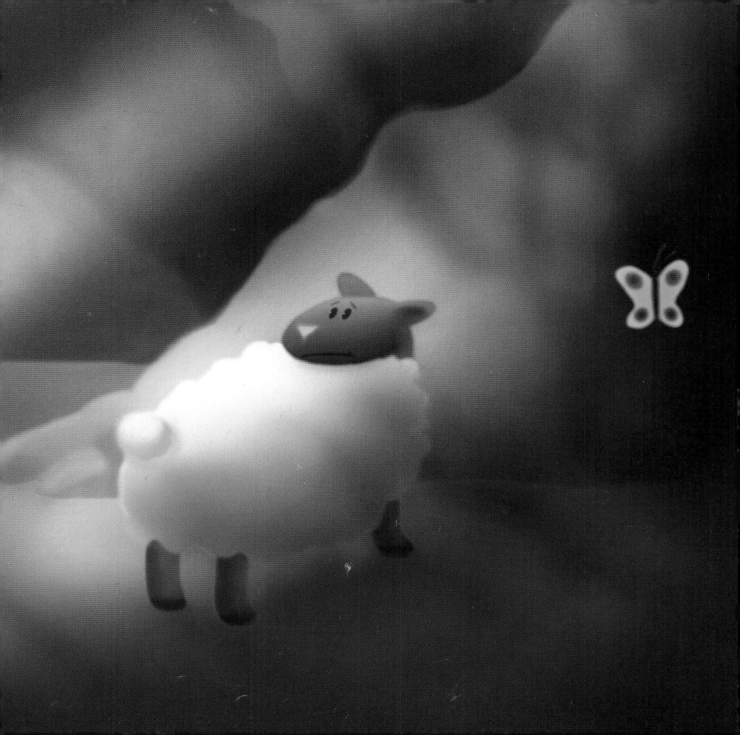

Even when I walk through the valley
of the shadow of death...

I will not be afraid.

You are close beside me,
protecting me and leading me.

You fix a delicious feast for me,
even when there is danger all around me.

You show me that I'm special!

Your goodness and love
will be with me
all of the days of my life.